MW01264174

STANDING IN THE BREACH

A PRIEST'S REFLECTIONS ON FAITH

W. Robert Abstein II

[signature]

THE PRESERVATION FONDATION, INC.

2313 Pennington Bend Road

Nashville, Tennessee 37214

Jacket painting by Rembrandt van Rijn (1606 –1669)

DEDICATION

To the women and men with whom I have shared this spiritual journey, I am grateful for the privilege of serving your parishes.

STANDING IN THE BREACH

Integrity or madness?

Standing in the breach…

Shepherding a flock

that no longer wants to be led.

"All we like sheep have gone astray…."

The certain laugh;

the fearful cry;

the doubters question.

But I must stand in the breach.

There is no other place to die.

Camp Solomon, Louisiana, 2010

AUTHOR'S PREFACE

Poetry has been very much part of my journey as a person of faith. It has always been a fascination for me. In my earliest years I read the Romantic poets— Keats, Wordsworth, and Coleridge. As an adult I read T.S. Eliot, Robert Frost and W. B. Yeats. I wanted to understand not only what the poet meant but also where the poet was leading me. I wrote many poems, most of them long since destroyed because I never felt they were worth sharing.

In the ordained ministry I found poetry to be a way to speak of the deepest things of the heart. Especially in times of stress, I found writing poetry to be one of the most helpful forms of expressing the tensions I felt.

The impetus for compiling this volume of poems written over several years comes from my experience at a long retreat where I was confronted with my feeling arising from a parish conflict over human sexuality. My fingers could hardly keep up with my long-suppressed thoughts as I allowed my feelings to emerge. It was as though I found my voice after a long period of silence.

I went back to my early journals where I had written poems and meditations on various occasions. I felt these, unlike my earliest writings, were worth sharing with others who have walked this faith journey. The life of faith has many twists and turns from times of being in wildernesses to discovering refreshing pauses at the wellspring of hope.

This book, <u>Standing In the Breach</u>, is a way of addressing the issues of one clergyman's role in living into the reality of proclaiming the gospel in all seasons. Some of these poems reflect the deep questions I have struggled with as I have journeyed with others in their pilgrimages of faith. There are doubts and convictions expressed, but also a deep hope that at journey's end I, too, will find the peace that was promised by our Lord.

The book is divided into four sections the first of which is **The Journey**. Like Abraham being called by God to travel to a place he knew not where, we journey through life seeking understanding and meaning. There are many questions along the way and often, I found, few concrete answers. There is tension between having faith and a certainty of faith that excludes all doubts. I have experienced the former but not the latter. These poems reflect that struggle.

The Challenge is the second section, which contains those poems that speak of the many challenges we face as we take this journey: to trust, to keep going at all costs, to suffer from being the shepherd in conflict, and to open our eyes to see and act in faith. To have faith without action is of little value. The challenge is to keep that balance between works and faith.

To Wrestle with Angels is the third section, which deals with some of the questions that I have encountered in my walk of faith. Like Thompson's "Hound of Heaven" I have tried running away only to return to face the pain of journeying in the wilderness. I have discovered that I cannot love or be loved without being vulnerable to that pain of betrayal and devotion. I wonder often why God would remain faithful to us when we are so unfaithful to God. Maybe that is the great rhetorical question in life.

The Journey's End—a New Beginning is the final section of this book. It reflects my hope that in this life there can be a sense of peace and joy as we journey in faith. Some of what I have found is the power of faith to live in the ambiguities or as the theologian, Paul Tillich, would say, "In spite of…" All of us have our "in spite of" moments. Mine have come in the renewal movements of our church, e.g. Cursillo and Faith Alive. These movements provided moments of reflection and joy even in seasons of struggle in the church. Like St. Peter who finds peace only after struggling with understanding the Christ he was following, I found comfort in knowing the shepherd of my soul was not going to leave me.

I concluded the book with a poem about Mary because she finds her role in the redemption story through her struggle to be the holy vessel for carrying God's son to the world. Like Mary I discovered the struggle is in fact a gift. It is the sign of God's call and God's promise to be with us always "in spite of" the struggles we face. She embraced her role in the drama of faith. We must do the same.

The drama does not end but continues for her and for us. When we understand this truth we understand that our journey's end is simply a new beginning of life found through Jesus.

My deepest thanks to Virginia Monroe, who encouraged me to share my poetry with others; John Magabgab, who helped me organize my thoughts and focus this small volume; and Kay Moser, who gave me valuable editorial advice. I am indebted to my wife, Roberta, my companion on this long and sometimes arduous journey in the ministry.

I used the New Heart English Bible translation for the scriptures quoted in the texts.

Bob Abstein

Lent, 2014

TABLE OF CONTENTS

THE JOURNEY

Where are we going?

Now the LORD said to Abram, "Get out of your country, and from your relatives, and from your father's house, to the land that I will show you."

Genesis 12:1

THE JOURNEY

Meditation on Psalm 121

Eyes lifted to the starry night
high above this wilderness…
a lone figure silhouetted
against a harvest moon standing
guard as a shepherd
protecting his flock.

The restless band of pilgrims gather
closer to the glowing fire.
Closeness brings feelings of comfort,
but nothing takes away the
fear that night brings
on their pilgrimage.

Eyes look hopefully beyond the guard

into the depths of space,

and from the depths of long journeys

into nights like this

a deeper question arises:

from whence does our help come?

Centuries later carnage of a broken

aircraft lies strewn over

a lonely Pennsylvania field…

tall buildings crumble from

brazen attacks…

a movie theater becomes a death trap

for those who only

wanted to see a film…

when simply going to work or play

becomes a day of infamy,

the question is repeated over and over again,

from whence does our real help come?

Bully taunts and electronic

venom spews forth

on gifted and beloved children,

who find solace only in suicide.

Once caring neighbors man

barricades and toss epithets

as easily as bombs

because skin color and head scarves

now divide.

Fear reigns and night threatens

to overcome us all.

From whence does our help come?

Lord, let me trust Your word

that light can overcome the darkness

that pervades my soul.

Give me the faith that claims

the hope of those

who journeyed in faith long before

this weary traveler—

that our help is in the

Name of the Lord.

Nashville, 2012

WAITING

The toad and I

Sat in the warm sun on the porch.

He was waiting for a meal

and I...

I was waiting for God.

Camp Solomon, Louisiana, 2010

ORTHODOXY

My self-image is in shreds

from confrontations with

those who are absolutely sure.

Defender of the faith?

I could be wrong.

But I could be right.

Left along the road

waiting for the wolves.

Camp Solomon, Louisiana, 2010

VICARIOUS WORSHIP

Dim lighting in the choir,
choristers process in
taking places at candle-lit stalls.
Their young voices intone Evensong
and we stand and listen.
Canticles are flawlessly sung
and we stand and listen.
Anthems ring out with angelic clarity
and we stand and listen.
My mouth urges me
to make liturgy
but I'm admonished
to allow my ears
and mind to do so.
Help me, Lord, to listen,

to hear the voices

of angels and archangels,

the saints: Augustine, Anselm,

Dunstan, Beckett

and listen and listen.

Calm my busy mind

that forces up words

before their time.

Let my soul speak to you

as a still small voice within

listening for Your still small voice without.

Canterbury, 1996

COMPASS ROSE

The nave floor etched and worn
by pilgrims' feet
pointing the way—a Compass—
but not true north.
It points us east to the altar
to Beckett's long absent crypt—

to Jerusalem.

It reads, "The truth shall set you free."

How difficult this journey

without a compass—

a clear-cut way.

Maybe the path is east

after all.

Canterbury, 1996

THE CHALLENGE

The obstacles we face

Even so faith, if it has no works, is dead in itself.
James 2:17

MORNING- BY- MORNING

Meditation on Isaiah 50:4-9

Morning by morning, Isaiah cries,
morning by morning God wakens his ear.
Not the sweet nothings of lover and beloved.
Those sweet words that
morning by morning
make the day by day worth sweat and toil.

No, not sweet nothings, but morning by morning
the clarion call to proclaim God's cry for justice:
God's claim on him, His spirit on him
to bring forth justice to the nations.

But this bringer of justice will be bruised
like a reed and burnt like a lamp wick—
bruised but not broken, burned but not consumed.

Small consolation for one whose life
is on the line.
But somehow sufficient for this burning prophet
held together by God,
to be a living promise to people
that God is faithful to those who believe.
God's servant—a suffering servant—
bruised by those who were incensed by his call
for justice and peace.
He came to share the refreshing word
for the weary.
But the weary turned against him—
They screamed in anger, "Speak no more!
Tell us no more!
We are weary with your word.
We don't want to be a light to others…
We want our share now
for us…just us!"
Walk the streets you know so well

and those you love walk to the other side

eyes averted.

You are a misfit:

a God-forsaken creature who claims

to hear God.

Children laugh.

A crazy man they say.

There's one in every town.

Battered down—a bruised reed—a flickering flame.

But every morning he rises to meet the day refreshed

for God has given him ears to hear

morning by morning his own Word.

Spoken from the beginning before time itself—

the dynamic word of creation.

The word of purpose that sees and understands

the relationship of frog and flower,

mosquito and asteroid,

sin and sinner.

A word that lives eternally within this created order.

The word of order, unity, wholeness,

and the word of forgiveness.

New is the day that begins

with that word

that calls him back

to that moment when

God and human stood together—at one.

To hear that Word is to know peace.

The darkness no longer fearful

for one has tasted peace and drunk from

justice's cup.

The pain of rejection no longer the destroyer.

The laughter comes back even in the darkest days

even with bruises and thorns.

Lord, I, too, hunger for that Word—

may it never fail me

morning by morning.

Nashville, 2002

GOD STOOD ABOVE THE CROSS

Meditation based on Genesis 22:2

Love, so short in length of line,

so deep in misunderstanding,

so trite to the shallow,

so unsatisfying to the greedy,

meaningless to those who grasp for its meaning.

Part 1

In the beginning, God.

Before all things God was,

and all things came to be through God.

Then God created man and it was good.

God took anger from the winds

that parch and dry the deserts.

God took violence from volcanoes

that rip blood red paths to the sea,

and God created man.

Then God created woman to live with man as one.

God took unlike nature from sea and shore.

God married the wind and rain together

to live as one...

and it was good.

But man's violent nature erupted

and his anger flowed.

He demanded equality with his creator.

But when all was said and done man stood alone...

separated from God...

separated from self.

And he ran the long road away from God.

God called but there was no answer.

God so loved the world God called him back,

but only the sound of frightened flight

could be heard.

Until in the land of Ur God called Abraham.

Was it because God so loved the world God told

Abraham to take his only son, Isaac,

whom he loved…

the child of his old age…

born long after Sarah had passed the time of

childbearing…

to offer him as a sacrifice?

Three days and nights Abraham took Isaac,

the wood, and the fire.

Each step taking them closer to Moriah,

where God was directing them.

Three days and nights to contemplate the pain

and agony of losing all that was good and beautiful

in his life.

And the question the boy asked carrying the wood,

"Where is the sacrifice?"

must have broken his heart.

"God will provide," was all Abraham could muster

as both made their way up that hill

from which, he thought, only one would return.

Did Isaac protest when his father bound him

and placed him on the altar?

Abraham drew his knife—

the blade flashing in the sun.

Only then did God step in…

Abraham passed the test.

He passed God's test

of righteousness.

He would not hold back anything

he held as his own,

not even treasure richer

than everything else he possessed—

his only son.

Yes, that, too, if God laid claim.

And that was good?

Part II

For God so loved the world, that he gave his one and only Son, that whoever believes in him should not perish, but have eternal life. John 3:16

Then God sent his own Son
as Abraham had sent his own flesh.
This time, the altar was made of wood,
and God stood above the cross
as Abraham had stood above the altar.

But God stopped Abraham.
He did not kill his son.
God had sent his Son in love,
which no one could possibly bear,
and God stood above the cross,
not stepping in and taking the nails
driven in by merciless hands,
and we in our own frailty must ask
was that love?
Yet, we read, "God so loved the world...."
Love, so short in length of line,

so deep in misunderstanding,

so trite to the shallow,

so unsatisfying to the greedy,

meaningless to those who grasp for

its meaning.

God sent his son to be the lover,

to woo us back to him.

We sought that love. We knew the lover.

And yet, in spite of it all,

the greatest lover died on a cross of hate

and somehow in the mystery of things,

God stamps an imprimatur in

just three words:

it was good.

Part III

Who can understand God's gift of life

bestowed on humankind?

Life that first requires a death,

a leap of faith into uncertainty when
one's only hope lies in the arms of Jesus.
A leap of faith,
a death to our own selfishness
and claims of equality with God—
a death to self…that we might live.
Who understands this kind of gift?

Who can understand the gift
that deals first a deathblow?
The act that gives abundant life from
apparently meaningless death?
And all of it from his own death
and only because of his death.
Who can truly understand?

God so loved you and me God gave his Son.
And yet to claim that love we must
accept God's call.
We find ourselves standing as if on the

edge of a great abyss

rallying our own courage to make

that leap of faith, to believe,

with not only the voice

of Jesus,

but the tempter, too, calling in our ears.

On the brink of death and faith we stand

trying to make that leap,

the leap of faith to Him below.

On this brink we stand crying out

our own fear saying "too far...

it's too far below."

We cannot see the bottom of the abyss,

but we do see how near the edge is.

We shrink back from our desire to leap

and the tempter rejoices all the more.

After all, let us be comfortable,

take one small step,

just one small step backwards.
Just one step backwards to be on safer ground;
one small step won't hurt.

But the tempter knows the tragic length
of that one step.
He knows how easy it is to turn.
He knows the hesitancy we have
to commit ourselves to that one leap.

With promises of powers and
kingdoms of our own
the tempter calls for us to turn
and take that one step back.
Take it…but was it good?
So we say, and so we do,
and because we have done it,
we proclaim:
it must be good!

It was taken, that one small step.

The ground is safer.

The edge is no longer near.

It is more comfortable here.

And a shroud keeps our shoulders warm.

In our frailty we cry,

"Is this not the same end to all?

The leap would have killed us, too.

Doesn't death, however it comes, have

the same drab meaning?"

So we say, and so we do,

and because we are safer,

it must be true.

But in those darkest hours we must confess

we have no hope.

Our old problem remains the same.

What if we'd dared to take that leap?

Would it have been the same?

Part IV

Abraham stood above the altar
but did not kill his Son.
And that was good.

God stood above the cross
but did not interfere
with the crucifixion of His Son.

God sent His Son with love
which no one could bear,
and God stood above the cross.
Finite man that I am—
infinite God that You are—
somehow, in the mystery of it all,
allow me to see
that I, too, may believe,
"It was Good."

Palm Sunday, 1966

ON SEEING

Sharing the Peace at the Sunday Eucharist
I exchanged greetings with a woman in a wheelchair on
my right.
After our greeting, she pointed
over her shoulder.
Behind the great pillar that had separated us
was another wheelchair-bound woman.
I reached for her hand.
She beamed with joy.
I had sat with her throughout the Eucharist
but had never seen her.
How many times do I not see others
for the barriers I've built over a lifetime?

Open my eyes, Lord, that I might see.
Canterbury, 1996

TENDING LOST SHEEP

The shepherd's coat is torn,

tattered from nights and days of toil:

lost sheep to be found,

ewes needing to birth,

and wolves' meals denied.

Piping notes to call them back

from death's door and loneliness.

Camp Solomon, Louisiana, 2010

THE FLOOD

The Harpeth, that benign stream-like
river wending its way through
scattered woodlands and alongside homes,
was now a raging torrent several miles wide
sweeping everything:
homes, trees, cars, outbuildings, and lives
into the Cumberland;
and even burying two of my friends
unceremoniously
behind a local market.

Rescue boats launched from city streets,
public boat ramps now thirty feet
below the river's surface,
hands wringing…,
cell phones no longer working,

anxiety levels raised to fear
for loved ones in the path
of creeks and streams turned to rivers of death
and destruction.

Standing on the bluff watching helplessly
as the river covers homes below.
A parking lot deemed above the flood level
becomes a lake with floating autos
parked there for safety…
alarms beeping until finally,
they, too, drown.

Aftermath…debris piles lined streets…
picture frames, which once held loved ones' photos
now look awkward lying next to sodden mattresses
and ruined wall board and insulation.
The smell of mold permeates the air.
Piles of rotting clothes
contaminated by all the pollutants
transported by the river resemble bodies

hoping for resurrection.

I am reminded of the debris piles
that litter the soul—
lies, deceit, sins committed openly or secretly.
These cannot be hauled away by city trucks
or decontaminated at the cleaners.
I can only lay them at the altar
and pray for peace,
for release
from the flood of memories
that continually bring
long-forgotten failures to light.

Not the Harpeth now…
but the heart.
Lord have mercy.
The current is too strong.
I cannot do this alone.

Nashville, May 2, 2010

THE NEW YEAR

Bright lights, festive shouts,

hugs and kisses abound,

glittering masks, Auld Lang Syne,

fireworks brighten rain-laden skies.

Resolves form on happy hearts

and Friday becomes Saturday,

a New Year.

Will more hungry children be fed

or peace reign from all those resolves?

Will fewer die of malaria

or fewer lie awake in refugee camps frightened of those

who steal childhoods by murder

and rape?

Glitter and confetti pile high in streets

from Berlin to Bombay,

New York to New South Wales,
and from hamlet to high-rise.

The sun rises on
a New Year of hopeful yearning
and the possibility of new life.
Or did Friday simply become Saturday…
Another day?

January, 2011

HOPE

"Jesus Christ is risen today, Alleluia!
Our triumphant holy day. Alleluia!" *
Thus rings out the familiar words
to the oft sung Easter hymn.
Most of these we can sing
without the hymnal…
at least one verse.

We are surrounded by familiar sights:
Easter lilies,
the vested choir,
white altar appointments.

It could be "business as usual,"
the same old thing.
But it is not.

There is a newness in the familiar;

there is the vitality of the rebirth

that overcomes all attempts

at being cast into a familiar mold.

This is Easter!

This is the Day of the Resurrection!

The Easter story is simple.

There is no need to repeat it again.

But there are a few things

that bear repeating:

there was a death and a burial;

there was genuine mourning;

there was an empty tomb, and

there was a reappearance and new life.

But above all there was rejuvenation and joy.

At the time of Jesus' crucifixion

there was not a spirit of "see you later."

It was ultimate and final.

It was real death and not some

"Mission Impossible" stunt.

The members of Jesus' tiny band were completely
undone
by all that had occurred.

Their confidence in each other was shaken.
Judas had betrayed their master.
Judas, with whom they trusted their money.
Peter had denied even knowing him.
Peter, the man they knew Jesus had called a rock.

The disciples were overcome by the experience of
the crucifixion.
Only later did any of this make sense.
Later, much later, did they understand
the necessity of it all.
And they were transformed by that knowledge—

They were made new by it.

….a will is in force where there has been death,

for it is never in force

while he who made it lives. (Hebrews 9:17)

Jesus died to restore the broken relationship

between God and humankind.

The price paid for this gift to humanity was death—

shedding of blood to seal the covenant.

The price was high,

but the benefit was even higher.

For through this gift, humanity has been given

the kingdom of heaven—

a new life…hope.

The spirit of Easter is the theme of new life.

Christ is risen!

Christ has conquered the fear of death,

that great enemy of humankind.

He took death and transformed it.

He made it a neutral factor,

a fact of life,

not something to be feared.

His death does not take away

the fact of death.

That is still with us.

But death is no longer the terminus;

it is now the entrance to a new life with him.

If we are to participate in this new life, we must share in

his death:

a death to selfishness and conceit,

a death to pride and prejudice,

a death to our anger and hatred,

a death to our indifference and apathy.

We must die to ourselves

if we are going to live with him.

That is the central message

of Easter for us today.

It is the same message heard by the disciples

two thousand years ago.

But we have not been transformed;
we have not all shared the experience of newness.
We have but to look around us:
the racist's bullet cutting down a man of God.

one who walked the way of righteousness;
the lists of dead and wounded fighting a war
that is tearing apart the fabric of our nation;
a group forming a militant nation
within our land by violent means;
young people struggling with their right to be free…
to be able to dissent from their parents…
but falling into new forms of dependence:
drugs…
alcohol.

Our nation's capital defended
by twice the number of soldiers
that were in Khe Sahn, Viet Nam, during the seige…

families teaching their children
racism under the guise of Christianity.

These are not the signs of life

or rebirth

or joy

or resurrection.

These are the signs of death.
Physical and spiritual death.

Death was Good Friday's theme;
it is not the theme for Sunday.
It is not the theme of today.

But these, too, can be made whole.
These signs can also be remade
in the image of God.

Christ led the way by giving up his life
that we might live.
The kind of living that forces you

out of the pews and into the cities

where life is truly being lived,
where people are existing on crumbs
and children are dying of hunger,
where oppressed blacks and whites
are enslaved by fear and frustration,
where hope is non-existent,
where hypocrisy is a fact
and morality a joke.

The action is where people are living and dying,
and we are called to be there.
The death of Christ is meaningless
if we are not transformed.
If we are not willing
to carry the cross

then we shall never taste
the new wine of life.
The sights and smell of death

permeate our society, our community,

yes, and even our church.

Has Christ died in vain?

Maybe we can awaken from our deathlike,

insensitive slumbers before it is too late.

Let us work to the end that this, too,

will be transformed by the Risen Lord,

so that we can truly sing and believe:

"Welcome happy morning,

age to age shall say.

Hell today is vanquished,

Heaven is won today" **

Let us not fall back to our old ways,

to the "business as usual" of everyday life.

Rather, let us take the living Spirit

out of the church with us

to share the rebirth with all

those for whom He died.

For He died that all of us

would be free.

Jesus Christ is Risen Today, Alleluia.

He has overcome death so that

we shall overcome its fear and be free.

Alleluia.

Decatur, Georgia, Easter 1968

*Hymn 207, The Hymnal 1982
** Hymn 179 The Hymnal 1982

WRESTLING WITH ANGELS

My Own Walk Of Faith

Jacob was left alone, and wrestled with a man [angel] there until the breaking of the day.

Genesis 32:24

PSALM 139

Where can I flee from Your presence?

I have found hell and wondered

why the unabated pain?

I have found the wilderness and fled…

the parched prayer remaining

on my swollen tongue and shriveled heart.

Is this where You wanted

me to be?

To find my breaking point?

Or to help me taste being alive?

Camp Solomon, Louisiana, 2010

OUR ISLAND HOME

Meditation on Psalm 8

When I consider your heavens,
the work of your fingers,
the moon and the stars, which you have ordained…

The vast heavens begin to reveal their secrets
as Hubble eyes deeper into her mysteries.
Blank spaces viewed by
earth-bound eyes
now reveal hundreds of millions more
galaxies, planets, and stars.

When I consider Your heavens
where do they end?

And when did they begin?
We can only stand in awe and wonder.

Who are we that You are mindful of us?
What gave rise to this creature
who can only bow
before the wisdom that
brought about our creation?

Who are we that You are mindful of us?
For we have not been
the caretakers of
"this fragile earth, our island home." *
Our plowshares have been turned back into
frightening weapons that can end
all that we are
or ever hope to be.
Our hearts have been turned from neighbor's care
to neighbor beware.

When I consider the work of
Your hands
and what we have done in return,

who are we that You

have not turned Your back

as we have surely turned ours?
Nashville, 2012

* "This fragile earth, our island home…"Book of Common
Prayer, p. 370

THE MENDING BASKET

Unmended jeans and shirts missing buttons
spilled from mother's mending basket in the hall
with promises made to right the wrongs
of careless play and aging wear.

Remembrances of broken promises and unmet needs
fill endless mending baskets
in the vast storerooms of my mind.
Heaps of clutter of past failures to live as
God would have me live
seem more, at times, than I can bear.

Soft kneelers in the creaking floor of the ancient church
do not comfort the hard veneer—

layer upon layer of protective coating

shielding the fearful soul inside

this penitent heart.

"You hate nothing you have made and

forgive the sins of all who are penitent..." *

How can God not hate the mess

we have made of so many things?

How can we ask forgiveness when there are

endless piles of unmended

clothes that can no longer cover up our

naked sins and failures,

the broken relationships we cannot mend?

"Remember you are dust" *

Job wallowed in the dust and ashes,

a broken man wishing never to have been born.

Ashes on the forehead...the sacred spot

of our baptism.

Lord, I know we are but dust and ashes,

but remembering that brings no joy.

"Have mercy on me, O God, according
to your loving kindness…" *
I cannot lift my head for the weight,
and I fear its loss would even
leave me without a heart.

"You look for truth deep within me…" *
There is comfort knowing You find
something deep within…even truth,
for often it feels like a wasteland,
a wilderness.
Settle my restless soul and tortured spirit
that I might know Your peace.

"Create in me a clean heart, O God…" *
I know I cannot do it on my own,
and I fall down at Your feet
from fear and sheer exhaustion
of running the race after my

own heart but never finding it.

I know if You but touch it,

I shall be clean and whole indeed.

Make me the heart I long to be

And revive the spirit that once was bright.

The bread—the Body...

I touch it knowing I am not

worthy to receive it.

Only by the sacred act of His love

it comes to me as a gift.

And I am grateful.

The taste of wine revives the heart.

I am refreshed by

remembrances of moments

when communion mended other lives

and brought healing to families

and longing hearts.

People made whole by the Blood of Christ.

I come to the altar knowing I am not

worthy of tying His sandals

but here in the chancel, the mystery of the

sacred meeting place,

I find a moment of peace.

This is my Body…given for you…

given for us.

And in the dust and ashes

I give thanks. Amen. Amen.

Ash Wednesday, 2012

*Ash Wednesday Liturgy,
Book of Common Prayer, pages 264-269.

THE JOUREY'S END—A NEW BEGINNING

Looking Forward In Hope

In the beginning was the Word, and the Word was with God, and the Word was God.
John 1:1

SAUL OF TARSUS

Saul was consenting to his death.   (Acts 8:1)

Saul stood resolutely looking on
as an outraged crowd threw young Stephen
into the pit.
A fitting punishment
for one who dared preach heresy
while addressing the learned Pharisees.
He'd dare preach this Jesus
against the God of Abraham.
Saul had agreed. Stephen should die.

Although this man was just the first
he knew many more would follow.
But at this moment,
he was disturbed by Stephen's dying words,

"Lord, do not hold this sin against them!"

Impressed always with any man's courage,

doubly impressed from one so young.

But not enough to stop the persecutions,

which soon spread like a raging fire.

But Saul ravaged the church, entering into every house,
and dragged both men and women off to prison.

Acts 8:3

Instead of being consumed by the conflagration,

the infant church spread

by those who fled the wrath of Saul.

Men and women seeking refuge

spread the name of Jesus Christ.

Praising God for their salvation

His word spread to every nation.

Saul, still breathing wrath and anger,

sought letters of passage

to seek the fleeing exiles in the city of Damascus

lest any should escape.

Soon his band began to approach

that famous city's imposing walls,

when he was stopped by a flash of light.

Its brilliance forced him to the ground.

His eyes shut in agony.

His companions were amazed

for they had seen nothing.

They were more amazed

when they heard sounds like someone speaking.

But Saul heard those words,

"Saul, Saul, why do you persecute me?" Acts 9:4

"Who art thou, Lord?" Saul replied,

groping in his world of darkness.

"I am Jesus," came the reply.

How can this be, he thought.

That same name evoked by Stephen.

The one they crucified on Calvary.

He's dead!

How can he be standing here in front of me?

Forcing open his eyes

to see this apparition
he was greeted by total darkness.
Those with him were confused at his behavior,
but seeing him blind
they led him by the hand
to the city they came to cleanse.

The gates of Damascus opened that day
for people of every kind:
merchants with their worldly goods,
wandering teachers and holy men,
simple peasants and city rulers.
Even some followers of Jesus
slipped in hopefully unnoticed by the zealous Jews,
who had already heard the news
that Saul was coming to search them out.
But those ancient gates
did not open for the fire branding avenger,
but a bewildered blinded man
in the midst of a crestfallen crowd.

For three days, Saul sat in darkness
trying to understand his fate.

His dreams tormented him
for over and over he saw
young Stephen kneeling in that hideous pit
forgiving those who hurled the pavement stones.

He saw the strong faces on weak people,
who went to death than defy
this man they called the Christ.
Surely Jesus could not be
the long expected one
for he was nailed upon the tree.
How did he know my name?
How could he have spoken
if he were dead?
Why am I blind and suffering so?

Amidst his plaguing dreams
he had visions of things to come.
He saw one coming to restore his sight.

If only this were true,
if only this could happen.

He saw himself again upon that road
where this nightmare had begun.
The sounds still lingered in his ears,

"I am Jesus, whom you are persecuting.
But rise up, and enter into the city,
and you will be told
what you must do." Acts 9:6

Crying out in the dark
he awoke thinking this was
but a dream
or some kind of trick

to keep him from his task.
But on waking the awful truth was still with him.
His eyes saw nothing.
In quiet desperation,
he turned to prayer

hoping there to find some peace.

No comfort did he find
among his friends
or those leaders from the synagogue,
who daily came to minister to his needs.
Peace came only when he addressed
the one he came to persecute,
"Jesus, hear my prayer."

On the third day in this lightless prison
one came to him whose name was Ananias.

Saul remembered his dreams
and questioned what all this meant.
He felt soothing hands upon his head;
something lifted from his eyes,

and he could see.
By the grace of God,
he was released from three days imprisonment
within himself.

Embracing Ananias, he wept for joy.
Both gave praise.
In the wake of this new life
Saul was baptized
in the name of the one
he sought to expunge

from the lips of all who believed in him:Jesus.
Sharing a meal together,
he was strengthened for what lay ahead.

Boldly he preached in the synagogue
that Jesus was the Son of God.

Fearing he was setting a trap,
the followers of Jesus fled from him.
The faithful Jews scorned him
and wondered at this change of heart.
But finding power in what he said,
Saul increased all the more in strength.
Escaping from a plot on his life
Saul left the city late one night.

In Jerusalem he joined with those
who had walked and talked with Jesus.

It was here he became Paul,
a new name for one who had been reborn.
The apostles shared with him
their understanding of this man
who lived briefly in their midst
and spoke to all of eternal life.

Overwhelmed by all he heard
and saw and felt
Paul retired to Egypt
that he might find himself;
his role in this new found faith.
Through prayer and meditations
Paul found some of what he sought;
that ultimately we only know forgiveness
when we live as though it is possible,
that it is true.
Only then do we discover

that Jesus from the cross
completely forgave
all that we have done.
Only as we live like forgiven people
shall we become whole.

It is this universal need we have,
the need to be made complete,
to know forgiveness,
which Christ answers from the cross,
and this became Paul's mission in life:
to preach the word of forgiveness
to all everywhere.
To preach that Jesus is the Son of God.

Like Mary, Paul had many doubts
about his worthiness to play
such an active role
in carrying out God's purposes for humanity.
But he accepted that unworthiness
and let God work through him.

Like Peter he had much in his past
for which he was ashamed.
But he accepted the words of Christ,

*"Father, forgive them, for they do not
know what they are doing."*

These words gave him strength
as he began his travels to the world.
He brought the good news
that we are no longer slaves,
but free people in Christ Jesus.
Paul found healing in his task
and new life within himself.
For as he ministered to others,
he felt a great one ministering to him.
And everywhere he went
he felt the presence of Christ,
touching him as he had done so long ago.

Paul could rejoice for in serving he was served,
in loving he was loved,

in giving he received,
and in dying he found eternal life.
All this from the hands of Jesus—
the Son of God.

Ash Wednesday, 1969

PETER

Based on Matthew 26:69-75

Peter wept bitterly.

Deep, painful tears of one who

knows firsthand the role of the denier.

Warm tears and the cold sweat of fear

glistened in that coarse beard,

which signaled manhood,

but now hid a coward.

If only he could die,

at least he would escape

the shame he felt

and the guilt he knew was his.

His life in shambles,

a foundering ship on the shoals.

All expectations shattered,

his hopes dashed.

What had seemed opportunity

now loomed before him a closed door.

Peter wept.

His mind charged,

a cornered animal,

there was no answer, no escape…

what was done was done.

Surely somewhere there was a reason

for saying to that harmless maid

he did not know the man.

Not merely once,

nor twice,

but three bitter times

he had denied the man he called his Lord.

His mind raced back to that first encounter,

brothers standing on the pebble-strewn shore

repairing nets from

the fruitless trip the night before.

Both had laughed at that teeming mass

of wild humanity

pressing against this wandering rabbi

now coming nearer.

Peter remembered the request

(or was it command?)

coming from this itinerant preacher

to use their boat

not to fish, not really fish,

but a pulpit for those lost souls.

After he finish speaking, he told them

to push out into the deep

and a harvest would be theirs.

Peter flashed a knowing smile to Andrew,

as if to say,

"Let's go along with this landlubber's game."

He told them to lower their nets.

Again he wondered, request or command?

It didn't matter for they

followed it in either case.

Maybe they were trying to prove him wrong,

or keep the peace,

maybe a little of both.

Into the deep their nets fell.

Suddenly the trailing lines groaned and

nets played out and stretched

until Peter feared they'd break.

They called upon James and John

to help them haul this mass they'd snared.

In their greed to fill their boats

they tipped as though

all would perish together.

Peter wept as he remembered

that struggle to keep the boats afloat.

"Even from the beginning I'd let him down.

Perhaps he should have let us drown.

But even then this wandering Jew,

who stepped into our midst unbidden,

already knew each of us."

By some power not yet apparent,

he saw to the core of Andrew, James and John.

"By some divine mystery, we ceased to be

just fishermen

and became his fishers of men.

We spent days and nights walking dusty roads

and talking to crowds who followed

wherever we went or stayed.

Long nights we spent listening,

but not always sure of what he thought

or what he meant by words uttered

with such grace."

"One such night I found the courage

to follow his command.

He appeared to us beside the boat

in the midst of a storm.

I cried above the howling east wind

that he should bid me come.

'Come,' he said and the power of his Word

steadied my trembling body

and I moved towards him.

I stood upon the violence of that raging sea.

I stood just as he stood,

and I glorified in my ability to stand.

And glorifying in my own power

I began to sink.

I cried for Him to save me!

Just as I have cried on

other nights such as this.

'Lord, save me from myself.

This self, which will not let me really follow you.

Lord, save me from this fearful body that stands
between my desire to follow and you.'"

Peter wept bitterly
as the crowing cock served notice.
He remembered what his Lord had said
that I would deny him three times.
"Somehow he knew and saw…
he knew what even I could not know,
what I could not see:
myself, as I really am."

It was not clear at first,
but came through the journey
with this man called Jesus.

Peter prided himself on being the first
to unravel the great mystery.
For he had grasped before the rest
the nature of the man they followed.

Jesus asked them once beside the road

who people thought he was.

Some replied that he was the Baptist

and others thought he was one of the great prophets:

Elijah or Jeremiah."

Jesus spoke again

with more urgency in his voice

wanting to know who we thought he was.

And no one spoke a word.

Suddenly words erupted from Peter

that he was The Christ of God.

In a moment of insight

he had touched the very nature

of the carpenter.

He was Christ, the Messiah.

The one anointed to restore a nation in captivity.

Jesus called him "Petras," a rock

on whom the church would be built.

But short lived was that glory, too.

Peter who seemed to understand the man

failed to comprehend the role he had to play.

He rebuked Jesus' words that he must die.

Surely, reasoned Peter, the Son of the living God

cannot be killed.

Confused and bewildered, Peter heard him say

that he was a hindrance, even the devil himself.

"A rock? On whom a church will be built?"

"Satan? A hindrance to the Son of God?"

"Lord, save me from myself!"

That last night after dinner

Peter, James, and John accompanied Jesus

to the garden to pray.

And there they waited with him.

He had been troubled and distraught.

But dinner and wine were too much to fight.

Devoted Peter, who was willing to die with Jesus,
slept while his friend passed through
that most difficult hour.
Finding them asleep, Jesus asked
could they not wait with him for just an hour?
Not even Jesus' pleading could keep open
their eyes that night.

But the alarm sounded.
The traitor, Judas, came and Peter rose to fight.
But Jesus held his arm
and kept him from using his sword.
They bound Jesus and took him away.
And James and John and all those with Jesus
fled like cowards into the night.

Peter wept bitterly when remembering
these past three years.
When called upon to live his faith,
his steps failed him.

His were the keys to the Kingdom of God,
but at this moment,
they could not even open his heart.

Not until that night.
For when the maid asked him if he knew Jesus,
Peter discovered fear.
He discovered he was afraid
for his own life.
The urge to preserve his own skin
was greater than the call to help.

Here with all of its sordid character
lay the center of his world,
within himself.
And he could not give that up.
He discovered what Jesus already knew,

he found himself.
Turning around, he met himself running.
He had followed Jesus for his own sake,

for his own glory,

for his own power.

And now in this darkest hour

he was exposed for what he was:

a coward, a fraud, a denier.

Christ he called master,

but fear was the master he served.

In that hour he prayed

as he had done when his boat was sinking;

as he had done when his faith had faltered.

He prayed as he had done when he was rebuked,

but now he prayed with his heart

full of understanding.

His simple prayer,

"Lord, save me."

He was right when he told her

that he did not know Jesus.

He did not know the man, but thought he did.

Now, in the night of his betrayal,

he found his Lord.

It was no longer fear he served.

He had finally found the One

who could save him from himself.

Amen

Ash Wednesday, 1969

THE PRODIGAL RETURNS

Reflections on Luke 15:11-32

A warm embrace,
the taste of tears on my face
but not my own.
The taste of love or grace?

A speech lost before
it is uttered
swallowed up by outstretched arms.

Is this an old man's need
to have his son home,
to bring him comfort in
his declining years?
Is this love….or grace?

Sometimes the longest step

is turning around.
The longest pause,
looking deep within.

I wanted freedom
but found a greater bondage
to the passions of my soul.

I longed for all that pleasure offered
but found only
the bitter taste of disillusionment
and despair.

Tears on my face,
my own,
the salty taste of insight.

Turning around this great
ship of fools
requires overcoming the fear
of acknowledging the truth,

one's own sin,

the failure to be.

Halting steps at first,

finding strength to move

in spite of inordinate fear.

Hope…to see my Father's face.

Fear…to find only closed doors.

Rightfully so.

But a long way off

a vision becomes reality—

the Father's face,

the Father's embrace,

never imagined hope fulfilled:

Grace.

Easter, 2012

WHEN STONES SPEAK

The celebrant stands dwarfed
as all others before him.
This place, this massive pile of stones
carefully crafted and carved,
skillfully laid
by generations now long gone.

The immensity of it
dazzles the mind
and causes me to ask
what love possessed them
who built it day by day
year by year?
The stones cry out
"Glory! Honor! Awe! Majesty!"
They dwarf our efforts to
fill this holy place with song.

Our best anthems are only a faint echo
to the anthems of these stones.
We sing out with humility
and leave records of our steps,
our knees,
in sloping risers and pavers
worn down by countless millions
coming to pay homage or gawk.

No sarcophagus present,
yet indentations around that vacant space
speak volumes
of ancient saints
who did obeisance to Thomas
martyred for his faith.

These stones speak
and echo our faintest prayers
with their resounding
AMEN.

Canterbury, 1996

93

MARY

A Meditation on Luke 1:26-31

PROLOGUE

The haughty misinformed neighbors
gathered round the well to tell their tales.

"Mary, poor Mary," they laughed behind her back.
Others soon joined this false-hearted chant,
"Mary, poor Mary.

Perhaps it was a wandering shepherd
who warmed her heart with glorious promises,
only to desert her
leaving her dreams dashed upon the floor."

"Mary, poor Mary," they said,
secretly gloating over hidden triumphs.

"Mary," they chanted, "how she longs for a husband,
but has none.
Now, poor thing," they snicker,
"she's expecting a child."

PART ONE

At an earlier time, in another place
her name was uttered with greater hope.
The angel of the Lord said to her
that she was not to be afraid
for she had found favor with God.
Be unafraid?
Be unafraid when addressed by a
messenger sent from God?
Do not be afraid when called upon by God
To do God's will?
The very idea evoked fear from the depths of her heart!
How can one so ordinary
find favor with God?
How can anyone find favor

with omnipotence?

Surely no stranger words could have been heard

by one so young

that she would bear a son.

"How can this be? I am but a virgin.

Surely God does not expect this of me!"

Mary, poor Mary, troubled not by the words of those

around the well,

but by those that penetrated the night air.

Simple Mary, who sought no glory on this earth,

trying desperately to find peace and understanding.

How comprehend a God who asks for all you have:

your reputation, your honor,

your chance for earthly happiness?

There was no greater shame than being with child

without the benefit of husband,

To be seen in the village as an unfit bride.

Cursed and condemned for indiscretion,

her only act was complete submission.

Words and more words filled her head,
that the Holy Spirit would overshadow her
and the child to be born to her
would be holy: the Son of God.
Words of hope, surely words of promise.
Were they too much for one whose only hope
was to know a husband?
So many words
they made the head swim and heart pound
with expectation and fear.
Yet she heard them clearly.
She was not be afraid for this child
will be called the God's Son.

"How can it be that God is calling me?
I do not seek honor or power or glory in this world.
Yet these promises—so lofty and noble,
so full of wonder—are so terrifying!"

How could it be that God wanted her?

Was this not just our neighbor, Mary?

An ordinary girl with modest dreams:

a warm bed to share with her intended;

a hearth to cook the meals she longed to fix;

a table to share the fruits of their toil;

and a home to fill with laughing children.

Yes, this was just our neighbor, Mary,

who wanted so little.

But called to be so much.

PART TWO

He will be great, and will be called the Son of the Most High. The Lord God will give him the throne of his father, David. Luke 1:32

Surely Mary knew the promises.

The rabbis spoke of the expected one.

She knew the role of God's Messiah.

Isaiah had said,

How beautiful on the mountains are the feet of him
who brings good news,
who publishes peace,
who brings good news of good,
who publishes salvation,
who says to Zion, "Your God reigns!"

Gabriel, the messenger, brought these tidings:
"Rejoice, you highly favored one! The Lord is with you!"

How strange the sound of these words
That she was the favored one.
Favored and yet to be the object of scorn
for those who do not believe.
But is there ever sufficient wisdom available
to believe a tale like this?
Or, for truly comprehending the divine will?
Who dares to reach out and touch
the Almighty's hand,
which is at this very moment resting

on the head of this youthful girl?

PART THREE

Mary arose in those days and went into the hill country with haste, into a city of Judah, and entered into the house of Zechariah and greeted Elizabeth.

Luke 1:39, 40

There is peace knowing you are not alone.

Especially on those nights when doubt and fear

replace the faith you hope for.

When even the noblest purpose has been ground down

into the bread for every day living.

There is comfort knowing

someone else shares your burden.

But to whom do you turn when your burden is as deep

as the mystery of God?

She turned to Elizabeth, a kinswoman,

who was also called to participate

in God's plan for humankind.

Chosen to give birth to one called John,

who would be called the forerunner,

a voice crying in the wilderness of human existence.

Elizabeth, poor creature, called to give this

birth in her old age;

but poor no more for she, too, was caught up

in the mystery and the excitement of the promise.

Elizabeth, filled with the Spirit of God,

exclaimed to Mary

that she was blessed among all women

as was the child in her womb.

Could she hear the words of her kinswoman,

or was the heaviness of her burden so great

she dared not understand their meaning?

Did she understand that it was her role

to carry within the softness of her flesh

the Son of God?

Did she feel the awful burden of knowing the greatness

that she alone had been chosen to nurture and protect?

More than a mere child, one who is indeed

more precious than all other gifts.

But a special child...to be born a babe and yet a king.

You who are blessed among women,

could you share your thoughts with Elizabeth?

Those shadows of realities to come?

Those deep-seated fears of how this child

would be accepted?

Does this not plague you, Mary?

Who could bear to hear words from God's own mouth?

If people rebel against the prophets,

mere spokespersons for God.

what shall they do to the Son of God?

Or, how shall they see him?

An oddity...a strange child?

Who but a woman knows

the anxiety of that moment before birth,

when all hopes and dreams focus on one central thought:

will my baby be whole?

Surely you also pondered this question, Mary:
will he be loved, or will the people find him
more than they can bear?
Elizabeth, could you hear the thoughts of Mary and
comfort her?
O sinful folk, can you bear the thoughts
of this simple girl?

PART FOUR

In the quietness of the night, Mary accepted her calling.
"See, the handmaid of the Lord; be it to me
according to your word."

And in her heart she spoke:
I submit myself to your word, Lord.
Be gentle for I am afraid,
be near for my quietness is not strength
but fear of my unworthiness.
There is no hint of glory or triumph in one who seeks

only to be the handmaid, not the mistress of the hall.
Humbly she submitted to the will of God:

Mary said, "*My soul magnifies the Lord.*
And my spirit rejoices in God my Savior,
for he has looked at the humble state of his servant girl.
For look, from now on all generations
will call me blessed.
For he who is mighty has done great things for me.
Holy is his name. Luke 1:47-49

Mary, whose soul took the leap of faith
not knowing where it would lead,
having only wild dreams and fearful expectations
of the role she would play, fully
entered the stage where the drama would take place.

It was a drama whose principal parts were already taken
assigned from creation—but not fully revealed.
Whose script consisted of merely a prologue:

In the beginning was the Word,
and the Word was with God,
and the Word was God.

EPILOGUE

The Word:

the power that gave courage and strength through the

words,

Do not be afraid, Mary, for the Word was made flesh

from your flesh

and because of you he dwelt among us.

The Word:

the earth trembled years later when the Word

was stretched upon the Tree to die

for the world he came to save.

The agony was there—

The pathos was there—

But triumphantly, the Word was there!

For the Word was made flesh for us:

to share our suffering,

to share our grief,

to raise us up into the divine image

in which we were created.

The Word was made flesh from flesh.

The handmaid of the Lord could now rejoice:

her role done, her sacrifice complete.

She fully accepted the divine commission:

Your will, not mine, be done.

The world looks back upon those events with ruthless

scrutiny.

And yet, nowhere do we hear the words:

"Mary, poor Mary."

But rather, "You who are blessed among women,

the Lord is with you."

For the promise was fulfilled:

a child was born.

He was named Jesus.

He was called holy,

for he is the Son of God.

Amen

Fourth Sunday of Advent 1980

Made in the USA
Charleston, SC
05 June 2014